Microwave
MAIN MEALS

**Compiled by Judith Ferguson
and Cecilia Norman
Edited by Delia Clark
Photography by Peter Barry
Designed by Philip Clucas
Produced by David Gibbon,
Gerald Hughes and Ted Smart**

CLB 1991
© 1987 Colour Library Books Ltd., Guildford, Surrey, England.
Text filmsetting by Focus Photoset Ltd., London, England.
Printed and bound in Barcelona, Spain by Cronion, S.A.
All rights reserved.
Published 1987 by Crescent Books, distributed by Crown Publishers, Inc.
ISBN 0 517 65297 8
h g f e d c b a

Microwave
MAIN MEALS

CRESCENT BOOKS
NEW YORK

Contents

FISH AND SEAFOOD

Codfish Pie

PREPARATION TIME: 15 minutes

MICROWAVE COOKING TIME: 11-12 minutes

SERVES: 4 people

4 cod fillets
2 tbsps lemon juice
2 tbsps water
1 bay leaf

SAUCE
3 tbsps butter
1 shallot, finely chopped
3 tbsps flour
1½ cups milk
2 tbsps chopped parsley
Salt and pepper

TOPPING
2 large potatoes, peeled and very thinly
   sliced
¼ cup grated Colby cheese
Paprika

Put the fillets in a casserole with the water, lemon juice and bay leaf. Cover loosely and cook for 2 minutes on HIGH. Melt the butter in a deep bowl for 30 seconds on HIGH. Add the shallot and cook for a further 1 minute on HIGH. Stir in the flour, milk, liquid from the fish, salt, pepper and parsley. Cook for 2-3 minutes on HIGH or until thick, stirring frequently. Pour over the cod. Slice the potatoes on a mandolin or with the fine blade of a food processor. Layer on top of the cod

Right: Codfish Pie (top) and Tuna, Pea and Fennel Casserole (bottom).

and season with salt and pepper. Cover the dish tightly and cook for 3 minutes on HIGH. Sprinkle on the cheese and paprika and cook, uncovered, for a further 2 minutes on MEDIUM to melt the cheese. Serve immediately.

Middle European Gratinee

PREPARATION TIME: 15 minutes	
MICROWAVE COOKING TIME: 14-16 minutes	
SERVES: 4 people	
TOTAL CALORIES: 842	

1 medium onion, peeled and finely chopped
6 medium tomatoes, skinned and chopped
1 tsp dry basil
Salt
Freshly ground black pepper
1lb whitefish fillet, skinned
1lb zucchini rinsed, topped and tailed and thinly sliced
2oz Monterey Jack cheese
2 tbsps fresh breadcrumbs

Put the onion into a bowl, cover and cook for 1 minute on HIGH. Stir in the tomatoes and basil and season with salt and pepper. Arrange layers of fish, onion mixture and zucchini in a shallow dish, finishing with a layer of zucchini. Cover and cook for 10 minutes on HIGH, turning the dish three times during cooking. Mix the cheese and breadcrumbs together and sprinkle over the zucchini. Without covering, cook for 3-5 minutes on HIGH or until the fish and zucchini are cooked. If the dish is flameproof brown under the broiler.

Tuna, Pea and Fennel Casserole

PREPARATION TIME: 15 minutes	
MICROWAVE COOKING TIME: 10 minutes, plus 10 minutes standing time	
SERVES: 4 people	

8oz green and whole-wheat noodles
1 cup frozen peas
1 small bulb Florentine fennel chopped
8oz can tuna, drained
3 tbsps butter or margarine
3 tbsps flour
¼ cup white wine
1¼ cups milk
Pinch oregano
1 small clove garlic, minced
Salt and pepper

TOPPING
Paprika
Parmesan cheese

Put the noodles in a large bowl with 3½ cups water. Cook for 6 minutes on HIGH and then leave to stand for 10 minutes. Drain, rinse under hot water, then leave to dry. Put the fennel into a casserole with 2 tbsps water. Cover and cook for 1 minute on HIGH. Drain and combine with the noodles, tuna and peas. Melt the butter for 30 seconds on HIGH with the garlic. Stir in the flour, wine, milk, oregano, salt and pepper. Pour over the noodles and mix well. Sprinkle on grated Parmesan cheese and paprika. Heat for 2 minutes on HIGH before serving.

Salmon in Chive Sauce

PREPARATION TIME: 15 minutes	
MICROWAVE COOKING TIME: 5 minutes	
SERVES: 4 people	

1 side of salmon (about 1½-2lbs)
2 tbsps butter or margarine
1 cup sour cream
½ cup light cream
1 tsp cornstarch
3 tbsps snipped chives
1 tsp coarsely ground black pepper
Salt

Slice the salmon horizontally into very thin slices. Heat a browning dish for 3 minutes on HIGH. Drop in the butter and heat for 30 seconds on HIGH. Lay in the salmon slices and cook for 30 seconds each side. Cook the fish in several batches. Remove the fish from the dish. Cover and keep warm. Mix the cream, sour cream, and cornstarch together. Pour into the dish and cook for 30 seconds on HIGH. Stir well and repeat the process until the cornstarch has cooked and thickened the sauce. The sauce should not bubble too rapidly, but the cornstarch will help prevent the sour cream from curdling. Stir in the chives, pepper and salt, and pour over the salmon slices. Serve with fine green noodles.

Halibut à la Normande

PREPARATION TIME: 15 minutes	
MICROWAVE COOKING TIME: 5-7 minutes	
SERVES: 4 people	

4 halibut fillets or steaks
½ cup white wine, dry cider or unsweetened apple juice
¼ cup water
1 tbsp flour
2 tbsps butter or margarine
1 shallot, finely chopped
2 medium-sized apples
¼ cup light cream
1 bay leaf
Salt and pepper
Lemon juice

GARNISH
Chopped parsley

Put the halibut into a casserole with the wine, cider or juice, water and bay leaf. Cover loosely and cook for 2 minutes on HIGH. Set aside and keep warm. In a small bowl melt half the butter. Add the shallot and cook, uncovered, for 1 minute on HIGH, stirring once. Peel and chop one of the apples. Add the shallot, cover the bowl loosely and cook for 2 minutes on HIGH, or until the apple is soft.

Facing page: Middle European Gratinee.

Stir in the flour, add the cooking liquid from the fish and heat for 2 minutes on HIGH. Stir the sauce twice until thickened. Add the cream and heat for 30 seconds on HIGH. Season with salt, pepper and lemon juice to taste. Heat a browning dish for 5 minutes on HIGH and drop in the remaining butter. Core and slice the second apple, but do not peel it. Brown the slices for 1-2 minutes on HIGH in the butter. Coat the fish with the sauce and garnish with the parsley. Serve surrounded with the apple slices.

Sole in Lettuce Leaf Parcels

PREPARATION TIME: 20 minutes

MICROWAVE COOKING TIME: 5 minutes

SERVES: 4 people

4 double fillets of sole or flounder
8 large leaves of romaine lettuce
8oz small shrimp
1 finely chopped shallot
½ cup chopped mushrooms
2 tbsps chopped parsley

This page: Sole in Lettuce Leaf Parcels. Facing page: Halibut à la Normande (top) and Salmon in Chive Sauce (bottom).

4 large caps canned pimento
1 cap pimento, chopped
½ cup white wine
½ cup heavy cream
1 cup low-fat soft cheese
Salt and pepper

Combine the shrimp, mushrooms, half the parsley, salt and pepper, and stuff the pimento caps with the mixture. Roll the fish fillets around the pimento and set aside. Put the lettuce leaves into a large casserole with 2 tbsps water. Cover tightly and cook for 30 seconds on HIGH to soften. Roll the leaves carefully around the stuffed fillets. Put seam-side down into a casserole with the wine and shallot. Cover loosely and cook for 3 minutes on HIGH. Remove the parcels and keep them warm. Cook the wine for a further 2-3 minutes on HIGH to reduce. Stir in the cream and bring to the boil for 2 minutes on HIGH. Add the cheese, salt, pepper, the remaining parsley and chopped pimento. Serve the sauce with the sole parcels.

Fruits of the Sea

PREPARATION TIME: 15 minutes

MICROWAVE COOKING TIME: 5-9 minutes

SERVES: 4 people

2lbs mixture of:
  raw scallops, cut in half
  raw shrimp, peeled
  1 lobster tail, shelled and cut into 1"
    chunks
  sole fillets, cut into 2" chunks
  oysters, shelled
  mussels, shelled
1 cup white wine
2 tsps cornstarch
1 tbsp lemon juice
½ cup whole-milk yogurt
2 tbsps chopped chives
8oz edible seaweed, soaked or cooked in
  2 tbsps water
Salt and pepper

Cook all the seafood in the wine for 2-3 minutes on HIGH. Cook the seaweed with 2 tbsps water for 1-2 minutes on HIGH. Mix the cornstarch and lemon juice. Remove the fish from the casserole and arrange on a serving dish with the seaweed. Combine the cornstarch and lemon juice with the cooking liquid from the seafood. Cook for 2-3 minutes on HIGH, stirring frequently until thickened. Add the yogurt and chives and heat through for 30 seconds on HIGH. Season with salt and pepper and pour over the seafood.

Fillets of Salmon with Peppercorn Sauce

PREPARATION TIME: 15 minutes

MICROWAVE COOKING TIME: 8-12 minutes

SERVES: 4 people

1 side of salmon, about 1½-2lbs
2 tbsps butter or margarine
1 cup heavy cream
⅓ cup dry vermouth
1 tbsp canned green peppercorns, rinsed
  and drained
Salt and pepper

Slice the salmon horizontally into very thin slices. Heat a browning dish for 3 minutes on HIGH. Drop in the butter and heat for 30 seconds on HIGH. Lay in the salmon slices and cook for 30 seconds each side. Cook the fish in several batches. Remove the cooked fish from the dish, cover it, and keep it warm. Pour the vermouth into the dish and add the peppercorns. Cook on HIGH for 2 minutes or until reduced by half. Add the cream, stir well, and cook for 2-3 minutes on HIGH until bubbling. Season with salt and pepper. Pour over the salmon scallops to serve. Serve with lightly cooked green beans or pea-pods.

Lychee Sole

PREPARATION TIME: 20 minutes

MICROWAVE COOKING TIME: 4-5 minutes

SERVES: 4 people

2lbs sole fillets
8oz lychees (canned or fresh), peeled
8oz can pineapple chunks, ½ cup juice
  reserved
Juice and rind of 2 limes
1-2 tbsps sugar
1 tbsp light soy sauce
2 tsps cornstarch
2 green onions, shredded
Salt and pepper

With a swivel peeler, peel strips off the limes, and cut into thin slivers. Cover well and set aside. Squeeze the lime juice, and mix with the pineapple juice, sugar, soy sauce and constarch in a small, deep bowl. Fold the fish fillets in half and place in a large casserole, thinner ends of the fillets towards the middle of the dish. Pour over enough water to cover ½" of the sides of the fillets. Cover the dish loosely and cook for 2 minutes on HIGH. Set aside and keep warm. Cook the sauce ingredients for 2-3 minutes on HIGH, stirring often until thickened. Add the cooking liquid from the fish, strained. Stir in the pineapple chunks, lychees, green onions and lime rind. Add a pinch of salt and pepper and pour the sauce over the fish. Serve with fried rice or chow mein noodles.

Sole Bonne Femme

PREPARATION TIME: 20 minutes

MICROWAVE COOKING TIME: 8-11 minutes

SERVES: 4 people

2lbs sole fillets
8oz whole mushrooms, stalks removed
4oz button or pickling onions, peeled
½ cup white wine
1 bay leaf

WHITE SAUCE
2 tbsps butter or margarine
2 tbsps flour
½ cup milk
Salt and pepper

BUTTER SAUCE
2 egg yolks
¼ cup butter
½ tbsp white wine vinegar
Salt and pepper

Facing page: Fruits of the Sea (top) and Fillets of Salmon with Peppercorn Sauce (bottom).

This page: Lychee Sole. Facing page: Sole Bonne Femme (top) and Salmon with Tomato Chive Hollandaise (bottom).

For the butter sauce, melt ¼ cup butter in a small, deep bowl for 30 seconds on HIGH. Mix the egg yolks, vinegar, salt and pepper together and beat into the butter. Have a bowl of iced water ready. Cook the sauce for 15 seconds on HIGH and beat well. Repeat until the sauce has thickened – about 1 minute. Put immediately into a bowl of iced water to stop the cooking. Set the sauce aside. Tuck the ends of each sole fillet under and place the fish into a large casserole. Add the mushrooms, onions, wine and bay leaf. Cover loosely and cook for 5-6 minutes on HIGH. Arrange the fish, mushrooms and onions in a clean casserole or serving dish and keep warm. In a small bowl melt the remaining butter on HIGH for 30 seconds. Stir in the flour, milk, cooking liquid from the fish, salt and pepper. Cook for 2-3 minutes on HIGH, stirring frequently until thickened. Beat in the butter sauce and pour over the fish to serve.

Salmon with Tomato Chive Hollandaise

PREPARATION TIME: 15 minutes

MICROWAVE COOKING TIME: 4 minutes

SERVES: 4 people

4 salmon fillets or tail portions
2 tomatoes, peeled, seeded and chopped
2 tbsps snipped chives
3 egg yolks
½ cup butter
1 tsp red wine vinegar
Salt and pepper

Poach the fish fillets in enough water to come half way up the side of the fillets. Cover loosely and cook for 2 minutes on HIGH. Keep warm. Beat the yolks with salt, pepper and chives. Add the vinegar and set aside. Melt the butter for 1 minute on HIGH in a small, deep bowl. Beat the yolks into the butter. Have a bowl of iced water ready. Put the sauce ingredients into the oven and cook for 20 seconds on HIGH. Stir and cook for 20 seconds more. Repeat until the sauce thickens – about 2 minutes. Put the bowl into the iced water to stop the cooking process. Add the tomatoes to the sauce and serve with the salmon fillets.

Curried Cod Nuggets

PREPARATION TIME: 15 minutes

MICROWAVE COOKING TIME: 7 minutes

SERVES: 4 people

2lbs cod, cut in 2" chunks
¼ cup lime juice
¾ cup water
2 tbsps butter or margarine
2 tbsps flour
1 large onion, chopped
1 tbsp curry powder
½ cup orange juice
2 oranges, peeled and segmented
2 tomatoes, peeled and seeded
Desiccated coconut

Combine the cod, lime juice and water in a large casserole. Cover loosely and cook on HIGH for 2 minutes. Set aside and keep warm. Melt the butter for 30 seconds on HIGH in a small, deep bowl. Add the onion, cover loosely and cook for 1 minute on HIGH. Stir in the curry powder and cook for 1 minute on HIGH. Add the flour, orange juice and cooking liquid from the fish. Stir well and cook, uncovered, for 2-3 minutes. Stir often until the sauce is thick. Slice the tomatoes into thin strips and add to the sauce with the orange segments. Cook the sauce for 10 seconds on HIGH to heat the orange and tomato through. Pour the sauce over the cod nuggets and sprinkle with desiccated coconut.

Salmon and Broccoli Fricassee

PREPARATION TIME: 20 minutes

MICROWAVE COOKING TIME: 10-12 minutes

SERVES: 4 people

2lbs salmon fillets or tail pieces
½ cup sliced almonds, toasted

This page: Salmon and Broccoli Fricassee. Facing page: Sea Bass and Fennel.

1lb broccoli
½ cup white wine
1 cup sliced mushrooms
1 tbsp butter
1 tbsp flour

1 cup chow mein noodles
1 tsp chopped dill
1 tsp chopped parsley
¾ cup cream
Salt and pepper

Put the fillets into a casserole with
enough water to barely cover. Cover
the dish loosely and cook for 2
minutes on HIGH. Reserve the
cooking liquid, flake the fish and set
aside. Put the broccoli into a bowl
with 2 tbsps water. Cover loosely and
cook for 4 minutes on HIGH. Drain
and arrange the broccoli in a
casserole with the flaked salmon.
Melt the butter in a small bowl for
30 seconds on HIGH. Stir in the
flour, cream, fish liquid and sliced
mushrooms. Cook for 2-3 minutes
on HIGH. Season with salt and
pepper. Add dill and parsley and
pour over the fish and broccoli.
Sprinkle over the almonds and
noodles. Heat through for 2 minutes
on HIGH before serving.

Sea Bass and Fennel

PREPARATION TIME: 15 minutes

MICROWAVE COOKING TIME:
23 minutes

SERVES: 4 people

1 sea bass, weighing 2-2¼ lbs, cleaned and
    trimmed
2 bulbs Florentine fennel
4 oranges
Juice of 1 lemon
1 tbsp anise liqueur
1½ cups whole-milk yogurt
Salt
Coarsely ground pepper

GARNISH
Samphire
Orange slices

Squeeze the juice from one of the
oranges and slice the others. Sprinkle
the inside of the bass with salt and
put it into a large, shallow casserole.
Pour over the orange juice and lemon
juice, cover and cook for 20 minutes
on HIGH. Carefully lift out the fish
and keep it warm. Cook the fennel in
2 tbsps water for 2 minutes on

HIGH and set aside. Stir the liqueur,
pepper and yogurt into the fish
cooking liquid and heat through for
30 seconds on HIGH. Do not let the
sauce boil. Peel the skin from the fish
if desired and pour over the sauce.
Garnish with the samphire and
orange slices to serve. Prepare with
other varieties of large whole fish if
desired.

Monkfish and Ribbons

PREPARATION TIME: 20 minutes

MICROWAVE COOKING TIME:
5-6 minutes

SERVES: 4 people

2 lbs monkfish tails
½ cup white wine
2 carrots, peeled
2 zucchini, ends trimmed
1 large or 2 small leeks, washed and
    trimmed, retaining some green
½ cup heavy cream
2 tbsps chopped parsley
½ tsp ground oregano
1 bay leaf
Salt and pepper

Cut the monkfish tails into ½"
rounds. Put the pieces into a
casserole with the wine and bay leaf.
Cover loosely and cook for 2
minutes on HIGH. Set aside and
keep warm. With a swivel vegetable
peeler, pare thin ribbons of carrot and
zucchini. Cut the leeks in half
lengthwise and then into ½" strips.
Put the vegetables into a small
casserole with 1 tbsp water. Cover
loosely and cook for 1 minute on
HIGH. Set aside. Remove the fish
from the casserole and heat the wine
for 2-3 minutes on HIGH to reduce.
Pour in the cream, and add the
oregano, salt and pepper. Heat
through for 30 seconds on HIGH.
Pour the sauce over the fish and
sprinkle on the chopped parsley.
Surround with the vegetable ribbons
to serve.

Right: Monkfish and Ribbons.

MEAT DISHES

Beef Roulades

PREPARATION TIME: 20 minutes

MICROWAVE COOKING TIME: 19 minutes

SERVES: 2 people

4 pieces rump steak, cut thin and flattened
1 dill pickle, cut into quarters lengthwise
2 green onions, trimmed and cut in half lengthwise
1 tbsp oil

SAUCE
½ cup mushrooms, quartered
1½ tsp butter or margarine
2 tsps flour
¼ tsp thyme
1 bay leaf
⅔ cup beef bouillon
1 tbsp red wine
Salt and pepper
Gravy browning (if necessary)

GARNISH
Buttered spinach pasta

Roll each of the beef slices around a quarter of the dill pickle and half a green onion. Sprinkle with pepper and fasten with wooden picks. Heat a browning dish on HIGH for 5 minutes. Put in the oil and add the roulades. Cook for 8 minutes, turning frequently. Remove from the dish and set aside in a casserole dish. Add the butter to the dish and allow to melt. Add the mushrooms and cook for 1 minute on HIGH. Stir in the flour and cook for 2 minutes to brown lightly. Add the bouillon, wine, thyme and bay leaf, scraping any sediment off the surface of the browning dish. Add gravy browning for extra color if necessary. Season,

and pour over the roulades. Cover the dish and cook for 12 minutes on MEDIUM. Test the meat with a knife and if not tender, cook for a further 3 minutes on HIGH. Serve with the pasta or French peas.
To serve one person, prepare only half the quantity of each ingredient and cook the roulades in the sauce for about 10 minutes on MEDIUM. Alternatively, the full quantity recipe freezes well.

Liver and Tomato Slaw

PREPARATION TIME: 15 minutes

MICROWAVE COOKING TIME: 14 minutes plus heating browning dish

SERVES: 4 people

TOTAL CALORIES: 1230

10oz white cabbage, finely shredded
1 small onion, peeled and finely chopped
1 carrot, peeled and grated
¼ cup natural low fat yogurt
1 tbsp horseradish sauce
1 tbsp low calorie mayonnaise/salad dressing
1 tbsp finely chopped parsley
1 tbsp vegetable oil
1lb lambs liver, trimmed and sliced
Salt
Freshly ground black pepper
8 tomatoes, sliced
1 tsp gravy powder

Mix the cabbage, onion and carrot in a large bowl. Combine the yogurt, sauces and parsley in a smaller bowl. Season the liver with salt and pepper. Preheat a large browning dish to maximum, add the oil and quickly brown half of the liver slices on both

sides. Remove them from the browning dish and set aside. Reheat the browning dish for 2 minutes on HIGH, then brown the remaining liver slices. Layer the liver slices and tomatoes in the browning dish or a suitable casserole, finishing with a layer of tomato. Sprinkle with the gravy powder. Cover and cook for 8-10 minutes on HIGH until the liver is just cooked. Cover and leave to stand for 5 minutes. Meanwhile cook the vegetables, uncovered, for 4 minutes on HIGH, stirring once. Stir the sauce into the warm vegetables and serve with the liver.

Lamb Chops with Currant Sauce

PREPARATION TIME: 5 minutes

MICROWAVE COOKING TIME: 6 minutes

SERVES: 4 people

TOTAL CALORIES: 760

4 4oz loin lamb chops, well trimmed
¼ cup currants
6 tbsps water
½ cup fresh brown breadcrumbs
Pinch ground cloves
2½ tbsp red wine
¼ tsp butter
Cooked green beans to garnish

Arrange the chops in a shallow dish or preheated, oiled browning dish, the bones towards the center. Cover with wax paper and cook for 2½

Facing page: Lamb Chops with Currant Sauce (top left) and Liver and Tomato Slaw (top right and bottom).

This page: Mixican Pork Casserole (top) and Beef Roulades (bottom). Facing page: Roast Beef with Stuffed Zucchini and Tomatoes.

minutes on HIGH. Place the currants in a bowl with the water, cover and cook for 2 minutes on HIGH. Add all the remaining ingredients, cover and cook for 1½ minutes on HIGH. Transfer the chops to a micro-proof serving dish and top each with the sauce. Cook uncovered for 5 minutes on LOW. Garnish with the green beans.

Mexican Pork Casserole

PREPARATION TIME: 15 minutes	
MICROWAVE COOKING TIME: 28 minutes	
SERVES: 2 people	

½ lb boneless pork loin, cut into 1″ cubes
½ cup canned garbanzo beans/chickpeas
½ cup canned kidney beans
¼ cup chopped sweet red pepper
¼ cup chopped green pepper
½ small chili pepper, finely chopped
¼ cup chopped onion
1 tbsp flour
2 tsps oil
¾ cup beef bouillon
1 tbsp instant coffee
½ clove garlic, crushed
¼ tsp ground cumin
¼ tsp ground coriander

GARNISH
Tortilla chips

Heat a browning dish for 5 minutes on HIGH. Put in the oil and add the pork cubes. Cook for 2 minutes on HIGH, stirring frequently, until slightly browned. Add the cumin, coriander, garlic, onion and flour, and cook for 1-2 minutes on HIGH. Dissolve the instant coffee in the bouillon and add to the casserole, stirring well. Add the peppers, cover, and cook on MEDIUM for 17 minutes, or until the pork loses its pink color. Add the beans and heat for 2 minutes on MEDIUM. Serve with tortilla chips if desired. To serve 1 person, prepare full quantity casserole, and freeze half.

Roast Beef with Stuffed Zucchini and Tomatoes

PREPARATION TIME: 20 minutes		

MICROWAVE COOKING TIME:		
Beef 14-21 minutes – rare		
16-24 minutes – medium		
18-27 minutes – well done		
plus 10 minutes standing time		

COMBINATION MICROWAVE CONVECTION TIME:		
Beef 10-12 minutes – rare		
11-13 minutes – medium		
12-14 minutes – well done		
Vegetables 13 minutes		

SERVES: 6-8 people

2-3lbs boneless beef roast
6-8 tomatoes
6-8 zucchini
4 tbsps chopped parsley
6oz mushrooms, roughly chopped
4 tbsps chopped chives
½ cup breadcrumbs
1 cup grated cheese
Salt and pepper

Put the beef, fat side up, into a large casserole, cover loosely and cook for 14-21 minutes for rare, 16-24 minutes

for medium, 18-27 minutes for well done on HIGH. Turn the beef over halfway through the cooking time. When cooked for the chosen amount of time cover with foil and leave to stand for 10 minutes before carving. The beef may also be cooked in a combination microwave and convection oven. Trim the ends of the zucchini and cook, in enough water to cover, for 5 minutes on HIGH. Cut in half lengthwise and scoop out the flesh, leaving the shell intact. Chop the flesh roughly and mix with the chives, salt and pepper. Fill the shells and sprinkle on the grated cheese. Cut the tops from the round end of the tomatoes, scoop out the seeds and strain the juice. Mix the mushrooms, tomato juice, parsley, breadcrumbs, salt and pepper. Fill the tomatoes and replace the tops. Cook the zucchini 5 minutes on HIGH and the tomatoes 3 minutes on HIGH, or until the vegetables are tender. Serve with the beef.

Lamb Hot-Pot

PREPARATION TIME: 15 minutes

MICROWAVE COOKING TIME:
30 minutes

SERVES: 4 people

2 large onions, peeled and thinly sliced
2 tbsps oil
1lb ground lamb
2 tbsps chopped parsley
Pinch thyme
8oz whole mushrooms
1 cup canned tomatoes
2 tbsps Worcestershire sauce
3 potatoes, peeled and thinly sliced
1 red pepper, cut in rings
1 green pepper, cut in rings
Salt and pepper

GARNISH
Fresh bay leaves

In a large casserole, heat the oil for 30 seconds on HIGH. Put in the onions and cover the casserole loosely. Cook 5 minutes on HIGH to soften the onions. Add the lamb and thyme and cook 10 minutes on MEDIUM, mashing the lamb with a fork to break it up while it cooks.

Add the mushrooms, tomatoes, parsley, salt and pepper and Worcestershire sauce. Arrange the slices of potato neatly on top of the lamb mixture and sprinkle with more salt and pepper. Cover the casserole and cook on MEDIUM for 15 minutes or until the potatoes are tender. Cook on a Combination setting of a microwave convection oven for 15 minutes or until potatoes are cooked and slightly browned. Three minutes before the end of cooking time, arrange the pepper rings overlapping on top of the potatoes. Garnish with fresh bay leaves to serve.

Glazed Ham and Spiced Peaches

PREPARATION TIME: 20 minutes

MICROWAVE COOKING TIME:
57 minutes, plus
5 minutes standing time

SERVES: 6-8 people

3lb ham, boneless and pre-cooked

GLAZE
2 tbsps Dijon mustard
½ cup dark brown sugar
1 cup dry breadcrumbs
Pinch powdered cloves
Pinch ginger

PEACHES
6 fresh peaches or 12 canned peach halves
½ cup light brown sugar
1 tsp each ground cinnamon, cloves and allspice
½ cup water or canned peach juice
2 tbsps cider vinegar
12 walnut halves

If using fresh peaches, put them into a large bowl and cover with boiling water. Heat on HIGH for 3 minutes or until the water boils. Peel the peaches, cut in half and remove the stones. Mix the remaining ingredients for the peaches together and heat 2 minutes on HIGH, stirring frequently until the sugar dissolves. Add the peaches and cook 2 minutes

on MEDIUM. Remove the peaches and cook the syrup a further 5 minutes on HIGH. Pour the syrup over the peaches and set them aside. Cover the ham with plastic wrap, or put into a roasting bag. Cook on MEDIUM for 15 minutes per lb. Pour the glaze over during the last 10 minutes of cooking. Put a walnut half in the hollow of each peach. Let the ham stand 5 minutes before slicing. Serve either hot or cold with the peaches.

Moroccan Lamb

PREPARATION TIME: 20 minutes

MICROWAVE COOKING TIME:
35 minutes

SERVES: 4 people

1¾ lbs lamb fillet or meat from the leg cut in 1 inch cubes
1 clove garlic, minced
2 tsps ground cinnamon
¼ tsp ground cloves
¼ tsp ground cumin
2 tsps paprika
1 large red pepper
2 cups light beef stock
¾ lb okra, trimmed
1 cup whole blanched almonds
¼ cup currants
1 tbsp honey
1 tbsp lemon juice
Salt and pepper

Combine the lamb, garlic, spices, red pepper, salt and pepper in a large casserole. Add the stock, cover the dish and cook on MEDIUM for 25 minutes. Add the okra, currants and almonds. Cook a further 5 minutes on MEDIUM. Remove the meat and vegetables and almonds to a serving dish. Add the honey and lemon juice to the sauce and cook on HIGH for 5 minutes to reduce it slightly. Pour over the lamb and serve with rice.

Facing page: Moroccan Lamb (top) and Lamb Hot-Pot (bottom).

Veal Escalopes with Vegetables

PREPARATION TIME: 20 minutes

MICROWAVE COOKING TIME:
20 minutes

SERVES: 4 people

4 veal cutlets
2 tbsps oil
2oz peapods
2 carrots, peeled and thinly sliced
2oz mushrooms, sliced
2 leeks, washed and thinly sliced
1 cup low-fat soft cheese
½ cup dry white wine
1 tbsp lemon juice

This page: Veal Escalopes with Vegetables. Facing page: Glazed Ham and Spiced Peaches.

1 tbsp chopped dill
Grated nutmeg
Salt and pepper

Heat a browning dish 3 minutes on HIGH. Add the oil and heat 1 minute on HIGH. Cook the veal for 8 minutes on HIGH. Add the mushrooms halfway through the cooking time. Combine the carrots and the leeks with the wine in a shallow dish and cook for 5 minutes on HIGH. Add the peapods and

cook a further 1 minute on HIGH. Drain the vegetables and reserve the liquid. Mix the cheese, vegetable cooking liquid, lemon juice, dill, nutmeg, salt and pepper in a deep bowl. Heat for 1 minute on HIGH, but do not allow the sauce to boil. Combine with the drained vegetables. Pour over the veal and heat through 1 minute on HIGH before serving.

Beef Bourguignonne

PREPARATION TIME: 20 minutes

MICROWAVE COOKING TIME:
53 minutes, plus
10 minutes standing time

SERVES: 4 people

2 thick-cut slices bacon cut in ½ inch
  strips
1½ lbs-2lbs chuck steak cut in 1 inch cubes
1 clove garlic, minced
8oz small onions
4 tbsps flour
1 cup Burgundy
1 cup beef stock
1 tsp tomato paste
8oz mushrooms, left whole
1 bay leaf
1 tsp thyme or majoram
Salt and pepper

Heat a browning dish for 5 minutes
on HIGH. Add the bacon and cook
3 minutes on HIGH, stirring
frequently until brown. Remove the
bacon and add the meat. Cook 3
minutes on HIGH to brown slightly.
Remove the meat and add the

onions. Cook 2 minutes on HIGH.
Stir in the flour, stock, wine and
tomato paste. Add the bay leaf, salt
and pepper. Return the bacon and
meat to the casserole and add the
mushrooms. Cover and cook
40 minutes on MEDIUM, or until
the meat is tender. Stir occasionally.
Leave to stand for 10 minutes before
serving. Serve with parsley potatoes.

Ham, Broccoli and Pineapple au Gratin

PREPARATION TIME: 15 minutes

MICROWAVE COOKING TIME:
10-12 minutes

SERVES: 2 people

4 slices cooked ham
8 broccoli spears

¼ cup sliced mushrooms
1 tbsp butter
4 pineapple rings, drained
2 tbsps water
Pinch of salt
1 tsp dark brown sugar

SAUCE
1 tbsp flour
1 tbsp butter
¼ tsp dry mustard
½ cup milk
2 tbsps shredded Cheddar cheese
Salt and pepper

TOPPING
¼ cup dry seasoned breadcrumbs

Put 1 tbsp butter in a small bowl and
cook for 30 seconds on HIGH. Add
the mushrooms and cook for
1 minute on HIGH and set aside. Put
the broccoli spears into a casserole
with the water and a pinch of salt.
Cover and cook for 4 minutes on
HIGH. Leave covered while preparing the sauce. In a 2 cup measure,
melt 1 tbsp butter for 30 seconds on
HIGH. Stir in the flour, mustard, salt
and pepper. Add the milk gradually
and cook on HIGH for 1-2 minutes,
stirring frequently until thick. Stir in
the cheese. Put 2 broccoli spears on
each ham slice, stalks towards the
middle, and top each with the
mushrooms. Roll up and put seam-
side down in a baking dish. Arrange
pineapple rings on each side and
sprinkle with the dark brown sugar.
Coat the cheese sauce over the
broccoli and ham rolls and top with
the crumbs. Cook on MEDIUM for
3-4 minutes or until hot. Serve
immediately.
To serve 1 person, make full quantity
sauce and cut all other ingredients to
half quantity. Cook the mushrooms
for 30 seconds on HIGH and the
broccoli for 3 minutes on HIGH.
Once assembled, cook for 2-3
minutes on MEDIUM. Left-over

**This page: Ham, Broccoli and
Pineapple au Gratin. Facing page:
Steak and Mushroom Pudding (top)
and Beef Bourguignonne (bottom).**

cheese sauce can be frozen, or kept in the refrigerator for 2 days. Bring to room temperature, re-heat on MEDIUM for 1-2 minutes to serve the sauce.

Steak and Mushroom Pudding

PREPARATION TIME: 25 minutes

MICROWAVE COOKING TIME:
51-52 minutes, plus
10 minutes standing time

SERVES: 4 people

PASTRY
2 cups flour
2 tsps baking powder
4oz shredded suet or ¼ cup butter or
    margarine
1 tsp salt
½ cup water

FILLING
8oz whole mushrooms
1lb chuck steak
2 tbsps butter or margarine
2 tbsps flour
1 small onion, finely chopped
1 cup beef stock
2 tsps chopped parsley
1 tsp thyme
Salt and pepper

Melt the butter in a deep bowl for 30 seconds on HIGH. Stir in the flour and the stock and cook for 1-2 minutes on HIGH. Add the remaining ingredients for the filling and cover the bowl loosely. Cook for 35 minutes on MEDIUM. Meanwhile, make the pastry. Sift the flour and baking powder and salt into a mixing bowl. Cut in the butter or stir in the suet. Mix to a soft dough with the water. Roll out ⅔ of the dough and line a 4 cup glass bowl, spoon in the filling and dampen the edges of the pastry. Roll out the remaining pastry for the cover. Place it over the top of the filling, pressing down the edges to seal well. Make 2-3 cuts in the top to let out the steam. Cover loosely with plastic wrap and cook on LOW for 15 minutes, turning the bowl around several times. Leave to stand for 10 minutes before turning out.

Liver Lyonnaise with Orange

PREPARATION TIME: 20 minutes

MICROWAVE COOKING TIME:
13-18 minutes

SERVES: 4 people

1lb liver, sliced
3 tbsps flour
2 tbsps butter or margarine
1 onion, sliced
Rind and juice of 1 orange
½ cup stock
Pinch thyme
Salt and pepper

GARNISH
Orange slices
Chopped parsley

Heat a browning dish 5 minutes on HIGH. Melt the butter in the dish for 1 minute on HIGH. Dredge the liver in the flour and add to the butter in the dish. Cook the liver for 1 minute on HIGH. Turn over and cook 1 minute further on HIGH. Remove from the dish. Cook the onions 1 minute on HIGH. Peel 1 orange and cut the peel into very thin strips. Squeeze the juice and add to the liver along with the remaining ingredients. Cook 10-15 minutes on MEDIUM, until the liver is tender. Turn the slices over frequently during cooking. Serve garnished with the orange slices and chopped parsley.

Risotto Stuffed Peppers

PREPARATION TIME: 20 minutes

MICROWAVE COOKING TIME:
20 minutes

SERVES: 4 people

2 large or 4 small red, green or yellow
    peppers
2 tbsps oil
1 small onion, chopped
1 clove garlic, minced

Right: Liver Lyonnaise with Orange.

1 cup Italian risotto rice
½ cup mushrooms
1 cup roughly chopped salami
¼ cup chopped black olives
8oz canned tomatoes
¼ tsp basil
¼ tsp oregano
1 cup mozzarella cheese, grated

Paprika
Salt and pepper

In a large casserole, cook the garlic, onion and mushrooms in the oil for 2 minutes on HIGH. Stir in the tomatoes, rice, herbs, salt and pepper. Cover the dish and cook on HIGH for 5 minutes. Stir in the meat and olives and leave to stand 5 minutes for the rice to continue cooking. If the peppers are small, cut 1 inch off the top to form a lid. Remove the core and seeds. If the peppers are large, cut in half lengthwise and remove the core and seeds. Fill the peppers and place them in the casserole. Cover with plastic wrap and cook 8 minutes on HIGH, until the peppers are just tender. Top with the cheese and cook 2 minutes on MEDIUM to melt.

Beef Enchiladas

PREPARATION TIME: 20 minutes

MICROWAVE COOKING TIME:
12-14 minutes

SERVES: 4 people

8oz package tortillas

SAUCE
1 onion, finely chopped
3 tbsps tomato paste
1lb 10oz can tomatoes
1-2 small chili peppers, seeded and finely
    chopped
1 tsp ground coriander
1 bay leaf
Salt and pepper
FILLING
2 tbsps oil
8oz ground beef
1 clove garlic, finely minced
2 tsps ground cumin
1 green pepper, roughly chopped
12 black olives, stoned and chopped
Salt and pepper

GARNISH
1 avocado, sliced
1 cup grated Cheddar or Monterey Jack
cheese

If the tortillas are dry, brush them with water, cover in paper towels and heat 2 minutes on HIGH before rolling up. Combine all the sauce ingredients in a deep bowl, cover the bowl loosely and cook 3 minutes on HIGH. Stir the sauce frequently to break up the tomatoes. If desired, blend the sauce until smooth in a food processor. Heat a browning dish for 3 minutes on HIGH. Pour in the oil and add the meat, breaking it up

This page: Risotto Stuffed Peppers (top) and Beef Enchiladas (bottom). Facing page: Pork Creole (top) and Sausages, Apples and Cheese (bottom).

with a fork. Add the garlic and cumin and cook on HIGH for 3 minutes, breaking up the meat frequently. Add the green pepper and cook a further minute on HIGH. Add the olives, salt and pepper. Roll up the filling in the tortillas and lay them in a shallow casserole, seam side down. Pour over the sauce and cook, uncovered, 1 minute on HIGH to heat through.

Top with the avocado slices and cheese and heat 1 minute further on HIGH to melt the cheese.

Sausages, Apples and Cheese

PREPARATION TIME: 15 minutes

MICROWAVE COOKING TIME:
10-12 minutes

SERVES: 4 people

1 ring smoked sausage
4 medium cooking apples, cored and
    thinly sliced
2 tbsp brown sugar
2 tbsp flour
1 shallot, finely chopped
1 tbsp chopped sage
1 cup shredded Cheddar cheese
Pinch salt and pepper

Toss the apples, brown sugar, flour, sage and onion together. Slice the sausage in ½ inch diagonal slices and arrange on top of the apples. Cover loosely and cook on HIGH 5 to 7 minutes or until the apples are tender. Sprinkle over the cheese and cook 5 minutes on Medium to melt. Serve immediately.

Pork Creole

PREPARATION TIME: 15 minutes

MICROWAVE COOKING TIME:
13 minutes

SERVES: 4 people

1 tbsp butter
1½ lbs lean pork shoulder or tenderloin cut
    into strips
1 clove garlic, finely minced
1 large onion, sliced
1 large green pepper, sliced
4oz mushrooms, sliced
1 tbsp tomato paste
2 tbsps molasses
8oz canned tomatoes
1 bay leaf
Pinch Cayenne pepper
Salt and pepper

Melt the butter in a casserole for 30 seconds on HIGH and put in the pork pieces, garlic, onions and

mushrooms. Cook 5 minutes on MEDIUM. Add the remaining ingredients and cook a further 5 minutes on MEDIUM, loosely covered. If the pork is not tender after 10 minutes, cook an additional 3 minutes on MEDIUM. Remove the bay leaf before serving.

Veal Ragout

PREPARATION TIME: 20 minutes

MICROWAVE COOKING TIME:
37-41 minutes, plus
5 minutes standing time

SERVES: 4 people

1½-2lbs veal shoulder or leg cut in 1 inch
    cubes
2 onions, sliced
8oz mushrooms, quartered
¼ cup butter or margarine
¼ cup flour
2 tsps thyme
1 bay leaf
1 clove garlic, minced
2 cups beef stock
2 tbsps tomato paste
Salt and pepper

ACCOMPANIMENT
3 cups pasta
1 cup grated cheese

Heat a browning dish 5 minutes on HIGH. Melt the butter 1 minute on HIGH. Brown the meat in 2 batches on HIGH for 3 minutes per batch. Cook the onions and mushrooms for 2 minutes on HIGH. Remove the meat and vegetables, and stir in the flour. Cook the flour for 3 minutes to brown slightly. Add the remaining ingredients and return the meat and the vegetables to the dish, or transfer to a casserole, cover and cook on MEDIUM 15 minutes. Put the pasta in water and partially cover with plastic wrap. Cook 6-10 minutes on HIGH, stirring occasionally. Leave to stand 5 minutes and drain and rinse in hot water. Remove the bay leaf from the ragout. Arrange the pasta in a serving dish and spoon the ragout into the middle. Sprinkle on grated cheese and heat 1 minute on HIGH to melt the cheese before serving.

Veal Involtini

PREPARATION TIME: 20 minutes

MICROWAVE COOKING TIME:
21-22 minutes

SERVES: 4 people

8 veal cutlets
8 slices Parma ham
8 slices cheese
2 tbsps chopped sage
Salt and pepper
2 tbsps oil

SAUCE
1 14oz can plum tomatoes
1 clove garlic, crushed
1 small onion, finely chopped
2 tbsps tomato paste
Pinch oregano
Pinch basil
Pinch sugar
1 bay leaf
Salt and pepper

Flatten the veal cutlets. Place on the ham and cheese and sprinkle on the sage, salt and pepper. Roll up, folding in the ends, and secure with wooden picks. Heat a browning dish 5 minutes on HIGH. Pour in the oil and heat 1 minute on HIGH. Add the veal rolls and cook 2 minutes, turning several times. Combine all the sauce ingredients in a deep bowl. Cook 3-4 minutes on HIGH. Remove bay leaf and blend in a food processor until smooth. Pour over the veal and cook, covered, on MEDIUM for 10 minutes. Serve with spinach.

Ham Loaf with Mustard Chive Sauce

PREPARATION TIME: 15 minutes

MICROWAVE COOKING TIME:
27-28 minutes, plus
5 minutes standing time

SERVES: 4 people

Facing page: Veal Involtini (top) and Veal Ragout (bottom).

¾ lb ground, cooked ham
¾ lb ground pork
½ cup dry breadcrumbs
½ cup milk
2 shallots, finely chopped
1 clove garlic, crushed
Salt and pepper

SAUCE
3 tbsps butter or margarine
3 tbsps flour
2 tbsps Dijon mustard
1 cup milk
½ cup light stock
2 tbsps chopped chives
Salt and pepper

Combine all the ingredients for the ham loaf and press into a glass loaf dish. Cook on HIGH for 5 minutes. Reduce setting to MEDIUM, cover with plastic wrap and cook 20-25 minutes, or until firm. Turn the dish after 10 minutes. Leave in the dish for 5 minutes before turning out to slice. Melt the butter for the sauce 30 seconds on HIGH. Stir in the flour and remaining ingredients, except for the chives. Cook 2-3 minutes on HIGH, stirring often until thick. Add the chives and serve with the ham loaf.

Spinach and Ricotta Stuffed Veal

PREPARATION TIME: 25 minutes

MICROWAVE COOKING TIME: 34-35 minutes

SERVES: 6 people

2-3lbs loin of veal, boned and trimmed
1 bay leaf
1 slice onion
1 cup stock or water

STUFFING
1lb fresh spinach, washed well
½ cup ricotta cheese
1 egg, beaten
2 tbsps pine nuts, roughly chopped
½ clove garlic, minced
1 tsp chopped basil
Grated nutmeg
Salt and pepper

SAUCE
Pan juices made up to 1½ cups with stock
2 tbsps flour
2 tbsps butter or margarine
2 tbsps dry white wine
Salt and pepper

Cook the spinach with 1 tsp water for 2 minutes on HIGH, in a covered bowl. Drain well and chop roughly. Mix the remaining stuffing ingredients with the spinach and spread on one side of the veal. Roll up from the thicker end of the meat to the thin end. Tie at even intervals with string. Place in a casserole with 1 cup water

or stock. Cover loosely and cook for 30 minutes on MEDIUM. Leave to stand 5 minutes before carving. Heat the butter 1 minute on HIGH and add the flour, stock, wine, salt and pepper. Stir to blend well and cook 2-3 minutes on HIGH, until thickened. Serve with the veal and a selection of vegetables.

This page: Spinach and Ricotta Stuffed Veal. Facing page: Ham Loaf with Mustard Chive Sauce.

Welsh Ham Rolls

PREPARATION TIME: 12 minutes

MICROWAVE COOKING TIME:
12-14 minutes

SERVES: 4-6 people

TOTAL CALORIES: 688

*1lb leeks, washed, trimmed and finely
    sliced*
⅔ cup salted water
Freshly ground black pepper
¾ cup cottage cheese
2 scallions, trimmed and finely sliced
1 egg
*6 1oz even shaped, lean, cooked ham
    slices*

Put the leeks and water into a
casserole. Cover and cook for
6 minutes on HIGH. Without
draining, purée in the food processor.
Season with pepper and add salt if
necessary. Spread the purée in a
shallow oval dish, and cook for 2-3
minutes on HIGH. Thoroughly mix
the cottage cheese, scallions with the
egg and pile a border of the mixture
along one edge of each ham slice.
Roll up and arrange on top of the
purée. Cover and cook for 4-6
minutes on HIGH. Serve hot.

Lamb in Sour Cream Dill Sauce

PREPARATION TIME: 15 minutes

MICROWAVE COOKING TIME:
31 minutes

SERVES: 4 people

2lbs leg of lamb, cut into 1 inch cubes
1 onion, sliced
1 bay leaf
1 tbsp dried dill or dill seed
1½ cups light stock
½ cup white wine
3 tbsps butter or margarine
3 tbsps flour
*2 tbsps chopped fresh dill or 1 tbsp dried
    dill*
½ cup sour cream
Salt and pepper

Make sure all the fat is trimmed from
the lamb. Put the lamb cubes, onion,

This page: **Welsh Ham Rolls.** Facing
page: **Lamb in Sour Cream Dill
Sauce (top)** and **Peppercorn Lamb
(bottom).**

bay leaf, dried dill or dill seed, salt,
pepper, stock and wine into a
casserole. Cover and cook on
MEDIUM for 25 minutes. Set aside
to keep warm. Melt the butter
30 seconds on HIGH. Stir in the
flour and strain on the stock from
the lamb. Stir well and cook for
5 minutes on HIGH, stirring
frequently, until thickened. Add the
dill, adjust the seasoning and stir in

the sour cream. Pour over the lamb
and heat through 1 minute on HIGH,
without boiling. Serve with rice or
pasta.

Peppercorn Lamb

PREPARATION TIME: 13 minutes

MICROWAVE COOKING TIME:
21-22 minutes

SERVES: 4 people

*1½ lbs lamb fillet or meat from the leg cut
    into ¼ inch slices*
4 tbsps butter or margarine
2 shallots, finely chopped

1 clove garlic, finely minced
3 tbsps flour
1 tsp ground allspice
1 cup beef stock
1 tbsp canned green peppercorns, rinsed
  and drained
2 caps pimento cut into thin strips
1 tsp tomato paste
¼ cup heavy cream
Salt and pepper

Heat a browning dish for 5 minutes on HIGH. Melt the butter for 1 minute on HIGH and add the slices of lamb. Cook for 2 minutes on HIGH, in 2 or 3 batches. Remove the meat and set aside. Cook the shallots and flour to brown slightly. Add the garlic, allspice, stock and tomato paste. Season with salt and pepper and cook 2-3 minutes on HIGH, until starting to thicken. Add the lamb, cover and cook 10 minutes on MEDIUM, or until the lamb is tender. Add the peppercorns, pimento and cream and cook for 2 minutes on HIGH. Serve with rice.

Polynesian Ham Steaks

PREPARATION TIME: 20 minutes

MICROWAVE COOKING TIME:
9-10 minutes

SERVES: 4 people

4 ham steaks
1 tbsp oil
1 small fresh pineapple, sliced
1 papaya, sliced
2 bananas, peeled and sliced
1 fresh coconut, grated
1 cup orange juice
Juice and grated rind of 1 lime
2 tsps cornstarch
2 tbsps brown sugar

Heat a browning dish 5 minutes on HIGH. Add the oil to the dish and lay in the ham steaks. Cook 2 minutes on the first side and 1 minute on the other. Set the ham aside. Combine the orange juice, lime juice and rind, cornstarch and sugar in a large bowl. Cook 1-2 minutes on HIGH, stirring frequently until thickened. Add the fruit and coconut and heat through 1 minute on HIGH. Pour over the ham steaks to serve.

Chicken Livers and Walnut Pasta

PREPARATION TIME: 15 minutes

MICROWAVE COOKING TIME:
13 minutes

SERVES: 4 people

1lb chicken livers, trimmed and pierced
¼ cup butter or margarine
1 clove garlic
½ cup walnuts, roughly chopped
1 cup stock
4 spring onions
2 tbsps chopped parsley

This page: Cranberry-Orange Ham Slices (top) and Polynesian Ham Steaks (bottom). Facing page: Chicken Livers and Walnut Pasta (top) and Kidney and Bacon Kebabs with Red Pepper Sauce (bottom).

1 red pepper, chopped
2 tbsps sherry
Salt and pepper
8oz pasta, cooked

Heat a browning dish for 5 minutes on HIGH. Melt the butter for 1 minute on HIGH and add the liver. Cook for 2 minutes on HIGH and add the garlic, salt and pepper and

stock. Cook 3 minutes on HIGH. Remove the livers from the stock and pour the stock into a food processor. Add the walnuts and blend until smooth. Chop the green onions and add to the sauce with the parsley, red peppers, and sherry. Pour over the livers and heat 2 minutes on HIGH. Pour over pasta to serve.

Cranberry-Orange Ham Slices

PREPARATION TIME: 10 minutes

MICROWAVE COOKING TIME:
7-9 minutes

SERVES: 4 people

4 ham steaks
1 tbsp butter or margarine

SAUCE
Juice and rind of 1 orange
8oz whole cranberry sauce
¼ cup red wine
1 tsp cornstarch
1 bay leaf
Pinch salt and pepper

GARNISH
1 orange, sliced

Heat a browning dish 5 minutes on HIGH. Put in the butter and brown the ham 2 minutes on the first side and 1 minute on the other. Combine sauce ingredients in a small, deep bowl. Cook 1-2 minutes on HIGH, until the cornstarch clears. Remove the bay leaf and pour over the ham to serve. Garnish with the orange slices.

Kidney and Bacon Kebabs with Red Pepper Sauce

PREPARATION TIME: 20 minutes

MICROWAVE COOKING TIME:
9 minutes, plus
1 minute standing time

SERVES: 4 people

16 kidneys
8 strips bacon
1 green pepper
¼ cup butter or margarine

SAUCE
2 tbsps dry mustard
2 tbsps Worcestershire sauce
2 tbsps steak sauce
2 large caps pimento
Salt and pepper

Pierce the kidneys 2 or 3 times. Cut the kidneys in half through the middle and remove the cores with scissors. Wrap the kidneys in bacon and thread onto wooden skewers with the green pepper. Melt the butter for 1 minute on HIGH and brush over the kebabs. Blend the sauce ingredients together with any remaining butter in a food processor until smooth. Cook the sauce 2 minutes on HIGH. Put the kebabs on a roasting rack and cook 5 minutes on HIGH, turning once. Leave to stand 1 minute before serving. Brush with the cooking juices before serving with the sauce. Saffron rice may also be served.

Sweet and Sour Ham

PREPARATION TIME: 20 minutes

MICROWAVE COOKING TIME:
2-3 minutes

SERVES: 4 people

1lb cooked ham, cut into ½ inch cubes

SAUCE
¼ cup brown sugar
¼ cup rice vinegar
2 tbsps tomato ketchup
2 tbsps soy sauce
1 can pineapple chunks, drained and juice reserved
2 tbsps cornstarch
1 green pepper, sliced
2 green onions, sliced diagonally
½ cup blanched, whole almonds
3 tomatoes, quartered
Salt and pepper

Combine the sugar, vinegar, ketchup, soy sauce, cornstarch and reserved pineapple juice and chunks. Add pepper, almonds, salt, pepper and ham. Cook 2-3 minutes on HIGH until the sauce clears and thickens. Add the tomatoes and green onions and heat 30 seconds on HIGH. Serve with rice or crisp noodles.

Speedy Ham Casserole

PREPARATION TIME: 10 minutes

MICROWAVE COOKING TIME:
6 minutes

SERVES: 4 people

8oz cooked ham, cut in ½ inch strips
1 can concentrated cream of mushroom soup
1 can water chestnuts, drained and sliced
2 sticks celery, finely chopped
8oz frozen, sliced green beans
2 tbsps dry sherry
1 cup light cream
Pinch thyme
Salt and pepper

TOPPING
1 can French-fried onions
or
¼ cup seasoned breadcrumbs mixed with 1 tsp paprika

Mix all the ingredients, except the topping ingredients, together in a serving casserole. Cook 5 minutes on HIGH, stirring occasionally, or until the beans have cooked. Sprinkle on the topping and cook a further 1 minute on HIGH.

Hazelnut Lamb

PREPARATION TIME: 15 minutes

MICROWAVE COOKING TIME:
25-30 minutes, plus
5-15 minutes standing time

SERVES: 6-8 people

4½ lbs leg of lamb
1 clove garlic, finely minced
1 cup dry breadcrumbs
1 cup ground, roasted hazelnuts
2 tbsps chopped parsley
¼ cup butter
Salt and pepper

Trim the fat off the lamb. Mix together the remaining ingredients except the breadcrumbs. Spread the

Facing page: Speedy Ham Casserole (top) and Sweet and Sour Ham (bottom).

hazelnut paste over the surface of the lamb and press over the crumbs. Cook 25-30 minutes on MEDIUM. Increase the setting to HIGH for 2 minutes. Cook 40 minutes on a Combination setting of a microwave convection oven. Leave the lamb to stand, loosely covered, 5 minutes before carving for rare. Leave 10-15 minutes if medium to well-done lamb is desired. Serve with minted new potatoes and peapods.

Veal Parmesan with Zucchini

PREPARATION TIME: 20 minutes

MICROWAVE COOKING TIME: 17-22 minutes

SERVES: 4 people

4 veal cutlets
4 zucchini

COATING
2 tbsps seasoned breadcrumbs
3 tbsps grated Parmesan cheese
1 egg, beaten
Salt and pepper

SAUCE
1 14oz can plum tomatoes
1 clove garlic, crushed
1 small onion, finely chopped
2 tbsps tomato paste
Pinch oregano
Pinch basil
Pinch sugar
Pinch grated nutmeg
1 bay leaf
Salt and pepper

TOPPING
1 cup mozzarella cheese
¼ cup grated Parmesan cheese

Slice the zucchini and cook 2 minutes on HIGH, with enough water to

cover in a deep bowl. Mix the crumbs, Parmesan cheese, salt and pepper for the coating. Dip the veal in the egg and then in the breadcrumb coating. Put the veal into a shallow dish, cover loosely and cook 8-10 minutes. Do not turn the veal over, but rearrange once during cooking. Combine all the sauce ingredients in a deep bowl. Cook 3-4 minutes on HIGH. Arrange the zucchini slices in a serving dish, place the veal on top of the zucchini and

This page: Hazelnut Lamb. Facing page: Veal Parmesan with Zucchini.

pour over the tomato sauce. Top with the mozzarella and Parmesan cheeses and cook 4-6 minutes on HIGH or Combination setting on a microwave convection oven. Serve immediately.

Microwave
MAIN MEALS

POULTRY AND GAME

Chinese Wings

PREPARATION TIME: 15 minutes

MICROWAVE COOKING TIME:
17 minutes

SERVES: 4 people

3lbs chicken wings
1 cup hoisin sauce (Chinese barbecue
* sauce)*
3 tbsps sesame seeds
2 tbsps vegetable oil
1 tbsp sesame seed oil
8oz peapods
8oz bean sprouts
Small piece grated fresh ginger root
Salt and pepper

Brush the chicken wings with the
hoisin sauce and cook for 10 minutes
on HIGH on a roasting rack. Baste
the chicken wings often with the
sauce while cooking. When the wings
are cooked and well coated with
sauce, sprinkle with sesame seeds and
set aside. Heat the oil in a browning
dish for 5 minutes on HIGH. Add
the peapods, bean sprouts, ginger,
salt and pepper. Cook for 2 minutes
on HIGH and add the sesame seed
oil after cooking. Serve the Chinese
wings with the stir-fried vegetables.

Quail with Apples and Calvados

PREPARATION TIME: 20 minutes

MICROWAVE COOKING TIME:
17-19 minutes

SERVES: 4 people

8 quail
2 large apples, peeled and thinly sliced
¼ cup butter or margarine

SAUCE
1 tbsp flour
½ cup white wine or cider
1 cup heavy cream
¼ cup Calvados or brandy
2 tbsps chopped parsley
Salt and pepper

Heat a browning dish for 5 minutes
on HIGH. Melt the butter and
brown the quail for 4-6 minutes,
turning often to brown evenly.
Remove the quail and set aside. Add
the sliced apples to the browning
dish and cook for 2 minutes, turning
over often to brown on both sides. If
the apples are not browning sprinkle
lightly with sugar. Remove the apples
and set them aside. Stir the flour into
the juices in the dish and add the
white wine and the Calvados. Return
the quail to the dish or transfer to a
casserole. Cover the dish tightly and
cook for 5 minutes on HIGH.
Remove the quail and keep warm.
Add the cream and the parsley to the
dish with salt and pepper. Cook for
1 minute on HIGH. Add the apples
to the sauce and pour over the quail
to serve.

Tandoori Poussins

PREPARATION TIME: 20 minutes,
plus 1 hour to marinate

MICROWAVE COOKING TIME:
15 minutes

SERVES: 4 people

4 Cornish game hens

MARINADE
½ cup chopped onion
1 small piece fresh ginger, grated
2 tsps ground coriander

2 tsps ground cumin
2 tsps paprika
1 tsp turmeric
1 tsp chili powder
1 cup plain yogurt
Juice of 1 lime
2 chopped green chili peppers
2 tbsps chopped chives
Salt and pepper

ACCOMPANIMENT
1 head of lettuce, broken into leaves
4 tomatoes, cut in wedges
1 lemon, cut in wedges

Combine all the marinade
ingredients together. Skin the hens
and cut them in half. Prick the flesh
and rub in the marinade. Leave for
1 hour. Cook on HIGH or a
Combination setting for 15 minutes,
basting frequently with the marinade.
Leave to stand, loosely covered, for
5 minutes before serving. Heat any
remaining marinade on MEDIUM
for 1 minute, but do not allow to
boil. Pour over the hens and serve on
a bed of lettuce with lemon and
tomato wedges.

Marmalade Venison

PREPARATION TIME: 15 minutes

MICROWAVE COOKING TIME:
40 minutes, plus
10 minutes standing time

SERVES: 4 people

2lbs venison, cut in 1 inch cubes
8oz small onions, peeled and left whole

**Facing page: Chinese Wings (top)
and Tandoori Poussins (bottom).**

Juniper Venison

PREPARATION TIME: 25 minutes

MICROWAVE COOKING TIME:
55 minutes, plus
10 minutes standing time

SERVES: 4 people

2lbs venison, cut in 1 inch cubes
¼ cup butter or margarine
¼ cup flour
2 cups beef stock
¼ cup red wine
1 shallot, finely chopped
1 sprig rosemary
1 tbsp juniper berries
1 bay leaf
Salt and pepper

ACCOMPANIMENT
1lb potatoes, peeled and cut into small
* pieces*
1 tbsp butter or margarine
1 egg, beaten
Salt and pepper
Rowanberry jelly, redcurrant jelly or whole
* cranberry sauce*

Cook the potatoes in enough water to cover for 15 minutes on HIGH. Leave to stand for 5 minutes before draining and mashing. Season the potatoes with salt and pepper and add the butter. Beat in half the egg and pipe the mixture out into small baskets on a plate or a microwave baking sheet. Cook for 1 minute on HIGH and then brush with the remaining beaten egg and sprinkle with paprika. Cook a further 2 minutes on HIGH and set aside. Heat a browning dish for 5 minutes on HIGH. Melt the butter and brown the meat and the shallot for 4-6 minutes on HIGH. Remove the meat and shallot and stir in the flour, stock, red wine, salt, pepper, juniper berries, rosemary and bay leaf. Return the meat to the dish or transfer to a casserole. Cover and cook for 30 minutes on MEDIUM, stirring frequently. Remove the bay leaf and the sprig of rosemary before serving. Reheat the potato baskets for 30 seconds on HIGH and fill each with a spoonful of the jelly or cranberry sauce. Serve the potato baskets with the venison. Garnish with fresh rosemary if desired.

¼ cup butter or margarine
¼ cup flour
2 cups beef stock
¼ cup orange marmalade

GARNISH
Orange slices
Chopped parsley

Heat a browning dish for 5 minutes on HIGH. Melt the butter and add the venison. Cook 4-6 minutes on HIGH, stirring frequently. Remove the meat and add the onions. Cook 1-2 minutes on HIGH to brown slightly. Remove the onions and add the flour, stock and marmalade. Return the meat and the onions to the casserole, cover and cook 30 minutes on MEDIUM. Leave to stand 10 minutes before serving. Garnish with orange slices and sprinkle with chopped parsley before serving.

This page: Juniper Venison (top) and Marmalade Venison (bottom). Facing page: Quail with Apples and Calvados (top) and Quail with Artichokes and Vegetable Julienne (bottom).

Turkey Korma (Mild Curry)

PREPARATION TIME: 15 minutes

MICROWAVE COOKING TIME: 10 minutes

SERVES: 1 person

1 turkey leg
2 tbsps chopped onion
1 tsp oil
1½ tsps butter or margarine
½ tbsp curry powder
1 tsp paprika
1 tsp ground coriander
1½ tbsps flour
½ cup chicken bouillon
1 tbsp golden raisins
1 tbsp roasted cashew nuts or shelled
   pistachio nuts
2 tsps unsweetened coconut
¼ cup plain yogurt
Salt and pepper

Skin and bone the turkey leg and cut the meat into 1″ pieces. Use half and freeze the other half for use later. Heat the oil in a large casserole for 30 seconds on HIGH. Add the butter and, when melted, add the onion, turkey and spices. Cook for 3 minutes on HIGH to cook the spices. Add the flour and bouillon and stir to mix well. Cover the casserole and cook for 5 minutes on HIGH, stirring frequently until the turkey is tender. Add the raisins, coconut, nuts, salt, pepper and yogurt. Leave to stand, covered, for 1 minute. Serve with rice and chutney.
To serve 2 people, use the whole turkey leg and double all other ingredients. Cook the casserole for 8 minutes on HIGH.

Quail with Artichokes and Vegetable Julienne

PREPARATION TIME: 25 minutes

MICROWAVE COOKING TIME: 19-21 minutes

SERVES: 4 people

8 quail
¼ cup butter or margarine
2 large artichokes, cooked
2 carrots, peeled
2 potatoes, peeled
2 leeks, washed

SAUCE
1 tbsp flour
½ cup white wine
1 cup heavy cream
2 tbsps Dijon mustard
Salt and pepper

GARNISH
Reserved artichoke leaves

Peel the leaves from the artichokes and remove the chokes. Set the leaves aside and cut the artichoke bottoms into thin slices. Cut the carrots, potatoes and leeks into julienne strips. Heat a browning dish for 5 minutes on HIGH. Melt the butter and add the carrots and potatoes. Cook on HIGH for 2 minutes. Add the leeks and artichoke bottoms and cook for a further 1 minute on HIGH. Remove the vegetables and set them aside. Add the quail to the butter in a dish and cook for 4-6 minutes on HIGH, turning frequently to brown lightly. Remove the quail from the dish and add the flour, white wine and Dijon mustard. Return the quail to the dish, cover tightly and cook for 5 minutes on HIGH. Set the quail aside to keep warm. Add the cream and salt and pepper to the dish and stir well. Cook for 1 minute on HIGH to thicken slightly. Add the vegetables to the sauce and cook a further 1 minute on HIGH to heat through. Pour the sauce over the quail to serve and surround with the artichoke leaves.

Fiery Duck

PREPARATION TIME: 15-20 minutes, plus 30-60 minutes to marinate duck

MICROWAVE COOKING TIME: 8 minutes, plus 1 minute standing time

SERVES: 2 people

½ a duck breast, boned and skinned –
   about ½ lb. If duck parts are
   unavailable, cut a whole duck into
   quarters and freeze the leg portions.
½ a small red pepper, sliced into ¼″ strips
2 sticks celery, thinly sliced
1 cup bean sprouts
2 green onions, sliced
½ cup roasted cashew nuts
½-1 tsp Szechuan pepper, or crushed dried
   chili peppers
½ tsp cornstarch
¼ cup chicken bouillon

MARINADE
2 tsps rice or cider vinegar
2 tsps soy sauce
2 tsps sherry
2 tsps sesame seed oil
Pinch ground ginger
½ clove crushed garlic
Salt and pepper

Remove the skin and bone from the breast portions and cut the duck into thin strips. Combine the marinade ingredients in a medium-sized bowl and stir in the duck pieces. Cover the bowl and chill for 30-60 minutes. Drain the duck, reserving the marinade, and mix the cornstarch, bouillon and Szechuan or chili pepper with the marinade. Put the duck into a large casserole and pour over sauce. Stir to mix, cover the dish and cook for 10 minutes on MEDIUM, stirring occasionally. Add the red pepper and celery to the casserole and cook for a further 2 minutes on HIGH. Stir in the cashews, onions and bean sprouts. Serve with fried rice or crisp noodles. Best prepared for 2 people.

Pheasant Alsacienne

PREPARATION TIME: 20 minutes

MICROWAVE COOKING TIME: 28-30 minutes

SERVES: 4 people

2 pheasants, dressed
2 onion slices
2 sprigs thyme
2 tbsps oil

Facing page: Fiery Duck (top) and Turkey Korma (bottom).

ACCOMPANIMENT
3 tbsps butter
3 tbsps flour
1 head white cabbage, shredded
2 apples, peeled and grated
2 tbsps caraway seeds
8oz smoked sausage, sliced
1 cup white wine
1 bay leaf
Salt and pepper

Prick the pheasants lightly all over the skin and brush with oil. Place the pheasants breast side down on a roasting rack, one at a time if necessary. Cook for 10 minutes on MEDIUM. Turn over and cook for a further 10 minutes on MEDIUM. Cook for 15 minutes on the Combination setting of a microwave convection oven, turning once. Cover and leave to stand while preparing the cabbage. Melt the butter in a large casserole for 30 seconds on HIGH. Add the flour and the wine and combine with the remaining ingredients. Cook for 8-10 minutes on HIGH, stirring frequently. Serve with the pheasants.

Stuffed Turkey Leg

PREPARATION TIME: 20 minutes

MICROWAVE COOKING TIME: 33-34 minutes

SERVES: 4 people

1 large turkey leg, bone removed

STUFFING
2 slices white bread made into crumbs
4oz cooked ham, finely ground
½ cup shelled pistachio nuts
1 apple, cored and chopped
2 sticks celery, finely chopped
1 shallot, finely chopped
Pinch thyme
1 egg, beaten
Salt and pepper

SAUCE
1 tbsp dripping from turkey
2 tbsps flour
Pan juices
1 cup chicken stock
2 tbsps dry sherry
Salt and pepper

GARNISH
1 bunch watercress

Combine all the stuffing ingredients and push into the cavity of the turkey leg, but do not overstuff. Close any openings with wooden picks. Prick the turkey skin lightly all over and put the turkey leg on a roasting rack. Cover loosely with wax paper and cook for 15 minutes on MEDIUM. Turn the turkey leg over and continue cooking on MEDIUM a further 15 minutes. Alternatively, cook 20 minutes on Combination in a microwave convection oven. When the turkey is tender and no longer pink, remove from the roasting rack and keep warm. Remove all but 1 tbsp of the fat from the roasting dish. Stir in the flour and add the chicken stock, sherry, salt and pepper. Transfer to a deep bowl if desired and cook 3-4 minutes on HIGH, stirring frequently until thickened. Slice the stuffed turkey leg and pour over some of the sauce. Garnish with watercress and serve the remaining sauce separately.

This page: Stuffed Turkey Leg.
Facing page: Pheasant Alsacienne.

Country Captain's Chicken

PREPARATION TIME: 20 minutes

MICROWAVE COOKING TIME: 36 minutes

SERVES: 4 people

3lbs chicken pieces
4 tbsps butter
2 tbsps curry powder
1 clove garlic, minced
1 large onion, sliced
½ cup blanched whole almonds
½ cup golden raisins
2 apples, peeled and diced
1 16oz can tomatoes
2 tbsps tomato paste
1 bay leaf
2 tbsps chopped coriander (optional)
Pinch sugar
Salt and pepper

GARNISH
Desiccated coconut

Heat a browning dish for 5 minutes on HIGH. Melt the butter and add the chicken pieces. Cook 15 minutes on both sides or cook in 2 batches for 7½ minutes each batch if necessary. Remove the chicken and add the onion, garlic and curry powder. Cook 1 minute on HIGH. Replace the chicken, skin side down, and add the raisins, apples and almonds. Mix the tomatoes, tomato paste, lime juice, coriander, bay leaf, sugar, salt and pepper together and pour over the chicken. Cook 15 minutes on HIGH, or until the chicken is tender and no longer pink. Turn the chicken over halfway through cooking. Remove the bay leaf and serve with rice and garnish with desiccated coconut.

Pigeon Kebabs with Walnut Grape Pilaf

PREPARATION TIME: 20 minutes

MICROWAVE COOKING TIME: 14 minutes

SERVES: 4 people

3-4 pigeons, depending on size
8 strips of bacon
2 tbsps butter or margarine, melted

WALNUT GRAPE PILAF
1½ cups brown rice
2 cups stock and wine mixed
2 tsps thyme
1 cup walnuts, chopped
1 small bunch purple or red grapes
Salt and pepper

Combine the rice with the stock and wine, salt, pepper and thyme in a large casserole. Cover loosely and cook for 10 minutes on HIGH. Cover completely and leave to stand 10 minutes for the rice to absorb the liquid. Add the chopped walnuts, cut the grapes in half and remove the seeds and add to the pilaf. Remove the breast meat from the pigeons and cut each breast half into 3 pieces. Thread onto skewers with the bacon. Brush each kebab with the melted butter or margarine and place on a roasting rack. Cook the kebabs 2 minutes per side. Set them aside, loosely covered, for 5 minutes before serving. Brush the kebabs with the cooking juices and serve on top of the pilaf.

Garlic Roast Pigeon

PREPARATION TIME: 20 minutes

MICROWAVE COOKING TIME: 15 minutes, plus 5 minutes standing time

SERVES: 4 people

4 pigeons
4 tbsps butter or margarine
12 cloves garlic, peeled
¼ cup white wine
1 cup chicken stock
1 bay leaf
1 sprig thyme
Salt and pepper

This page: Country Captain's Chicken. Facing page: Pigeon Kebabs with Walnut Grape Pilaf (top) and Garlic Roast Pigeon (bottom).

ACCOMPANIMENT
4 heads Belgian endive
1 cup water and white wine mixed
Pinch sugar
Salt and pepper

Spread the butter on the pigeons and place them breast side up on a roasting rack with the cloves of garlic. Cook on HIGH or a Combination setting for 10 minutes. Leave the pigeons to stand for 5 minutes before serving. They may be served slightly pink. Meanwhile, mash the cloves of garlic and mix with the stock, wine, bay leaf and salt and pepper. Cook, uncovered, for 3 minutes to reduce the liquid. Purée the sauce until smooth. Cut the endive in half lengthwise and remove the cores. Put into a casserole dish with the wine and water mixed, sugar, salt and pepper. Cover loosely and cook for 2 minutes on HIGH. Drain and serve around the pigeons. Pour the sauce over the pigeons and the endive to serve.

Turkey Macadamia

PREPARATION TIME: 20 minutes

MICROWAVE COOKING TIME:
18 minutes

SERVES: 4 people

4 turkey breast cutlets
1 (8oz) can pineapple chunks, juice
*   reserved*
4 green onions, sliced
4 tomatoes, peeled, seeded and quartered
1 cup macadamia nuts

SAUCE
2 tbsps soy sauce
1 cup stock
2 tbsps vinegar
2 tbsps brown sugar
3 tsps cornstarch
Reserved pineapple juice

Place the turkey breasts in a casserole dish and pour over the pineapple juice. Cover the dish tightly and cook 10-15 minutes on MEDIUM. Leave to stand while preparing the sauce. Drain the pineapple juice from the turkey and combine it in a deep bowl

with the remaining sauce ingredients. Add the pineapple pieces and the macadamia nuts. Cook, uncovered, for 2-3 minutes on HIGH, stirring frequently until thickened. Immediately add the tomatoes and the onions to the hot sauce and pour over the turkey to serve.

Orange Glazed Duck

PREPARATION TIME: 15 minutes

MICROWAVE COOKING TIME:
40 minutes

SERVES: 3-4 people

4½-5lbs duck
1 slice orange
1 slice onion
1 bay leaf
Salt

GLAZE
¼ cup bitter orange marmalade
4 tbsps soy sauce
1 cup chicken stock
2 tsps cornstarch
Salt and pepper

GARNISH
Orange slices and watercress

Prick the duck all over the skin with a fork, brush some of the soy sauce over both sides of the duck and sprinkle both sides lightly with salt. Place the duck breast side down in a roasting rack. Cook 10 minutes on HIGH and drain well. Return the duck to the oven, reduce the power to MEDIUM and continue cooking a further 15 minutes. Combine remaining soy sauce with the orange marmalade. Turn the duck breast side up and brush with the glaze. Continue cooking for 15 minutes on MEDIUM, draining away the fat often and brushing with the glaze. Remove the duck from the roasting rack and leave to stand, loosely covered with foil, for 5 minutes before carving. Alternatively, cook 20-25 minutes on Combination in a microwave convection oven. Drain all the fat from the roasting tin, but leave the pan juices. Combine the chicken stock, cornstarch, salt, pepper and remaining glaze with the

pan juices and pour into a small, deep bowl. Cook 2-3 minutes on HIGH until thickened. Remove the onion, orange slice and bay leaf from the cavity of the duck and put in a bouquet of watercress. Surround the duck with orange slices and serve the sauce separately.

Duck with Peaches

PREPARATION TIME: 20 minutes

MICROWAVE COOKING TIME:
9 minutes

SERVES: 4 people

2 whole duck breasts
¼ cup butter
Salt and pepper

SAUCE
2 cans sliced peaches, drained and juice
*   reserved*
½ cup red wine
2 tsps cornstarch
1 tbsp lime or lemon juice
1 bay leaf
Pinch cinnamon
Pinch nutmeg
1 tbsp whole allspice berries
½ cup whole blanched almonds

Heat a browning dish for 5 minutes on HIGH. Melt the butter and put in the duck breasts. Brown the duck breasts 2 minutes on the skin side and 4 minutes on the other side. Remove from the dish and leave to stand while preparing the sauce. Mix the cornstarch with the peach juice, red wine, lemon juice and the spices and bay leaf in a deep bowl. Cook on HIGH for 2-3 minutes until thickened. Remove the bay leaf and add the peaches. Slice the duck breast into thin slices. Pour the peach sauce over the duck breasts to serve.

Facing page: Turkey Macadamia (top) and Duck with Peaches (bottom).

MEALS WITHOUT MEAT

Vegetable Moussaka

PREPARATION TIME: 55 minutes

MICROWAVE COOKING TIME:
29 minutes

SERVES: 4 people

2 potatoes, peeled and sliced
1 eggplant
4oz mushrooms sliced
2 zucchini
4 tomatoes, peeled and sliced
1 green pepper, sliced

TOMATO SAUCE
1 tbsp oil
1 onion, finely chopped
1 clove garlic, minced
1 14oz can tomatoes
1 tbsp tomato paste
¼ tsp ground cinnamon
¼ tsp ground cumin
Salt and pepper
Pinch of sugar

EGG SAUCE
2 tbsps butter or margarine
2 tbsps flour
1 cup milk
1 egg, beaten
½ cup feta cheese
Nutmeg
Salt and pepper

Cut the eggplant in half and lightly
score the cut surface. Sprinkle with
salt and leave to stand for ½ hour.
Put the potatoes into a roasting bag,
seal and cook 10 minutes on HIGH.
Heat the oil for the tomato sauce 30
seconds on HIGH. Add the onions
and garlic and cook 1 minute on
HIGH. Add the remaining
ingredients and cook a further 6
minutes on HIGH. Wash the
eggplant well and dry. Slice it thinly
and cook in 2 tbsps oil for 2 minutes
on HIGH in a covered dish. Remove
the slices and drain. Add the
mushrooms to the dish and cook for
2 minutes on HIGH. Remove and set
aside. Add the green pepper and the
zucchini and cook for 1 minute on
HIGH. Layer the vegetables, starting
with the eggplant and ending with
the potatoes. Spoon the tomato
sauce over each layer except the
potatoes. Cook the butter for the egg
sauce for 30 seconds on HIGH. Stir
in the flour, nutmeg, salt and pepper.
Add the milk gradually and cook for
3 minutes on HIGH, stirring after
1 minute. Add the cheese and egg
and stir well to blend. Pour over the
potatoes and cook 4 minutes on
HIGH or 5 minutes on a
combination setting in a microwave
convection oven, or until set.

Mushrooms Florentine

PREPARATION TIME: 20 minutes

MICROWAVE COOKING TIME:
17 minutes

SERVES: 4 people

¼ cup butter or margarine
1lb large mushrooms
2lb fresh spinach, stalks removed and
　leaves washed
2 shallots, finely chopped
4 tomatoes, peeled, seeded and diced
Salt and pepper
Nutmeg

SAUCE
3 tbsps butter or margarine
3 tbsps flour
2 cups milk
1½ cups grated Cheddar cheese
½ tsp dry mustard
Pinch cayenne pepper
Salt and pepper
¼ cup Parmesan cheese, grated
Paprika

Place the washed spinach in a large
bowl or roasting bag with a pinch of
salt. Cover or seal and cook 4
minutes in the water that clings to
the leaves. Set aside. Melt the butter
in a large casserole for 30 seconds on
HIGH. Cook the mushrooms for
3 minutes on HIGH, turning often.
Remove the mushrooms and set
them aside. Add the shallots to the
butter in the bowl, cover, and cook
2 minutes on HIGH. Chop the
spinach roughly and add to the
shallots with the tomato, salt, pepper
and nutmeg. Place in the bottom of
the casserole dish and arrange the
mushrooms on top. Melt the butter
for the sauce 1 minute on HIGH. Stir
in the flour, mustard, salt, pepper and
a pinch of cayenne pepper. Add the
milk gradually, beating until smooth.
Cook, uncovered, 4 minutes on
HIGH, stirring twice after 1 minute's
cooking. Add Cheddar cheese and
stir to melt. Coat over the
mushrooms and spinach and sprinkle
the Parmesan and paprika on top.
Cook 3 minutes until bubbling.

Pasta Primavera

PREPARATION TIME: 20 minutes

MICROWAVE COOKING TIME:
14 minutes plus 10 minutes
standing time

SERVES: 4 people

**Facing page: Vegetable Moussaka
(top) and Mushroom Florentine
(bottom).**

SERVES: 4 people

2 cups navy beans
¼ cup oil
2 cloves garlic, minced
2 small leeks, cut in 1 inch pieces
3 carrots, cut in 1 inch chunks
4 sticks celery, cut in 1 inch pieces
2 parsnips, halved, cored and cut in 1 inch
    pieces
2 turnips, peeled and cut in 1 inch pieces
4oz mushrooms, quartered
1 tbsp Worcestershire sauce
1 bay leaf
1 tbsp marjoram, chopped
1½ cups vegetable stock
Salt and pepper

TOPPING
2 tbsps butter or margarine
½ cup dry breadcrumbs

Heat a browning dish for 5 minutes on HIGH. Melt the butter for the topping and add the crumbs. Stirring frequently, cook on HIGH for 2-3 minutes until the crumbs are golden brown and crisp. Set them aside. Add the oil to the browning dish and heat for 1 minute on HIGH. Add all of the vegetables and cook 2 minutes on HIGH to brown. Stir frequently. Remove the vegetables from the browning dish and de-glaze the dish with the vegetable stock. Stir to remove any sediment from browning the vegetables. Cover the beans with water and leave to soak overnight or microwave for 10 minutes to bring the water to the boil. Allow the beans to boil for 2 minutes. Leave them to stand for 1 hour. Drain the beans and put them into the casserole dish with the garlic, bay leaf, Worcestershire sauce, marjoram, salt and pepper. Add half the stock, cover and cook for 1 hour on HIGH. Add more stock as necessary during cooking. The mixture should be fairly thick at the end of the cooking time. Add the vegetables and re-cover the dish. Cook an additional 15-20 minutes on HIGH, adding more

6 cups pasta shapes, or noodles
8oz asparagus
4oz green beans
2oz mushrooms, sliced
2 carrots
3 tomatoes peeled, seeded and cut in
    strips
6 green onions
2 tbsps chopped parsley
2 tsps chopped tarragon
½ cup heavy cream
Salt and pepper

Cook the pasta 6 minutes on HIGH in 4 cups hot water with a pinch of salt and 1 tbsp oil. Cover and leave to stand 10 minutes before draining. Leave to drain completely. Slice the asparagus diagonally, leaving the tips whole. Cut the beans and carrots diagonally into thin slices. Cook the

carrots and asparagus in 2 tbsps water for 4 minutes on HIGH, loosely covered. Add the beans and mushrooms and cook an additional 2 minutes on HIGH. Add to the drained pasta and stir in the cream, salt and pepper. Cook 1 minute on HIGH to heat the pasta. Add the tomatoes, onions, herbs and toss gently. Cook an additional 1 minute on HIGH. Serve immediately with grated cheese if desired.

Vegetable Cassoulet

PREPARATION TIME: 20 minutes
MICROWAVE COOKING TIME:
1 hour 40 minutes plus indicated standing times

This page: Pasta Primavera. Facing page: Chinese Black Bean Casserole (top) and Vegetable Cassoulet (bottom).

stock if necessary. When the beans are tender and most of the liquid has been absorbed, sprinkle on the brown crumbs and cook for 5 minutes on HIGH. Leave the cassoulet to stand for 15 minutes before serving. The cassoulet may be prepared in advance and refrigerated. Re-heat 2-3 minutes on HIGH. Add the crumbs and cook a further 5 minutes on HIGH before serving.

Curried Vegetables

PREPARATION TIME: 20 minutes

MICROWAVE COOKING TIME: 17 minutes

SERVES: 4 people

2 medium-size potatoes, peeled and cut into 1 inch chunks
3 carrots, cut into 1 inch chunks
3 zucchini, sliced
4oz okra, stems trimmed
2oz mushrooms, quartered
2 tomatoes, quartered
1 large onion, sliced
3 tbsps oil
1 clove garlic, minced
1 red or green chili pepper, minced after removing the seeds
2 tbsps flour
1 tsp ground cumin
1 tsp ground coriander
1 tsp turmeric
2 tsps mustard seed
½ tsp paprika
Pinch ground cloves
Bay leaf
2 cups vegetable stock or vegetable cooking liquid and water
½ cup natural yogurt
Salt and pepper
GARNISH
Chopped coriander leaves

Cook the potatoes and carrots together in a large, covered casserole. Add just enough salted water to cover the vegetables. Cook on HIGH for 8 minutes. Add the zucchini and okra after 6 minutes cooking. Leave the vegetables to stand, covered, for 5 minutes. Reserve the quartered tomatoes and mushrooms. Heat the oil for 1 minute on HIGH and add the onion, garlic, chili pepper and mushrooms. Cook for 1 minute on

HIGH. Stir in the flour and spices and cook a further 1 minute on HIGH. Add the liquid gradually, stirring until smooth. Add the bay leaf, salt and pepper and cook 5 minutes on HIGH, stirring frequently after 1 minute. When thickened, remove the bay leaf and add the cooked vegetables and the quartered tomatoes. Heat through 1 minute on HIGH. Serve with rice and chutney. The accompaniments from the Curried Lentil recipe may also be served.

Chinese Black Bean Casserole

PREPARATION TIME: 20 minutes

MICROWAVE COOKING TIME: 1 hour 33 minutes plus indicated standing time

SERVES: 4 people

1lb black beans
1 small piece fresh ginger root, grated
1 clove garlic, minced
2 tsps 5-spice powder
1 piece star anise
6-8 sticks celery
1 small can water chestnuts, drained and sliced
⅓ cup sherry
1 tbsp soy sauce
1 tsp sesame seed oil

GARNISH
4oz bean sprouts
4 green onions shredded

Cover the beans with water and leave to stand overnight, or microwave on HIGH for 10 minutes to boil the water. Allow the beans to boil for 2 minutes and leave to stand for 1 hour before using. If using salted Chinese black beans, soak in cold water for ½ hour and drain. Cut the cooking time in half. Cover the beans with water and add the grated ginger, star anise, 5-spice powder and garlic. Add a pinch of salt and pepper and loosely cover the bowl. Cook for 1 hour on HIGH, stirring occasionally. Add the celery and cook a further 15 minutes on HIGH. Add the sherry, soy sauce and sesame oil

and cook a further 5 minutes on HIGH. If a lot of liquid remains, continue to cook until the liquid is absorbed. Add the water chestnuts just before serving and cook 1 minute on HIGH to heat through. Garnish with the bean sprouts and shredded green onion to serve.

Gratin of Vegetables Oliver

PREPARATION TIME: 20 minutes

MICROWAVE COOKING TIME: 12-13 minutes

SERVES: 4 people

TOPPING
½ cup butter or margarine, melted
1 cup chopped, pitted black olives
1 cup dry breadcrumbs
1½ cups shredded Cheddar cheese
1 cup chopped walnuts
2 tsps chopped fresh basil
Pinch cayenne pepper

VEGETABLES
4 zucchini, sliced
1 bunch broccoli
4 carrots, sliced
8oz green beans
2 red peppers, sliced
8 green onions, sliced
Salt and pepper

Melt the butter for the topping for 30 seconds on HIGH. Stir in the remaining ingredients and set aside. Cook the carrots in 4 tbsps water with a pinch of salt for 8 minutes. After 5 minutes add the zucchini, broccoli and beans. Add the peppers and green onions 1 minute before the end of cooking time. Drain the vegetables and arrange in a serving dish. Sprinkle lightly with salt and pepper and sprinkle over the topping ingredients. Bake 4 minutes on MEDIUM or 5 minutes on a combination setting in a microwave convection oven. Serve immediately.

Facing page: Gratin of Vegetables Oliver (top) and Curried Vegetables (bottom).

Red Beans Creole

PREPARATION TIME: 20 minutes

MICROWAVE COOKING TIME:
1 hour 23 minutes plus standing
times indicated in the recipe

SERVES: 4 people

1 cup red kidney beans
1½ cups long-grain rice
2 tbsps butter or margarine
1 green pepper, cut in strips
3-4 tomatoes, peeled, seeded and cut in strips
4oz mushrooms, sliced
4 green onions, chopped
2 tbsps chopped parsley
Cayenne pepper
Ground nutmeg
1 bay leaf
Salt and pepper

Cover the beans with water and
leave overnight, or microwave 10
minutes to boil the water. Allow the
beans to boil for 2 minutes. Leave to

**This page: Red Beans Creole. Facing
page: Japanese Steamer.**

stand 1 hour. Cover with fresh water
and add a pinch of salt and the bay
leaf. Cook on MEDIUM for 55
minutes to 1 hour. Allow to stand
10 minutes before draining. The
beans must be completely cooked.
Save the cooking liquid to use as
stock in other recipes if desired. Place
rice in a large bowl or casserole dish,
add 2 cups water and a pinch of salt.
Cook about 10 minutes on HIGH.
Leave to stand for 5 minutes before
draining. Heat the butter or
margarine 30 seconds on HIGH in a
casserole dish, and add the pepper
strips and mushrooms. Cook for 2
minutes, stirring once. Stir in the
cayenne pepper, nutmeg, salt, pepper,
rice and beans. Cook 1 minute on
HIGH. Add the green onions, parsley
and tomatoes and cook a further 30
seconds on HIGH.

Japanese Steamer

PREPARATION TIME: 20 minutes

MICROWAVE COOKING TIME:
13 minutes

SERVES: 4 people

3 packages tofu, drained
16 dried black mushrooms, soaked and stems removed
4oz small mushrooms
8 baby corn-on-the-cob
1 small daikon (mooli) radish, sliced
1 bunch fresh chives, left whole
4oz buckwheat noodles or other variety Japanese noodles
1 package dried sea spinach
1 lemon, sliced

SAUCE
1 small piece fresh ginger root, grated
½ cup soy sauce
4 tbsps vegetable stock
1 tbsp sherry or white wine
1 tsp cornstarch

Cover the noodles with 2 cups water
and a pinch of salt. Cook on HIGH
for 6 minutes and leave to stand,
covered, for 10 minutes before using.
Put the mushrooms and spinach into
2 separate bowls, fill both bowls with
water and leave the spinach to soak.
Put the mushrooms into the
microwave oven and heat for
5 minutes on HIGH and set aside.
Put the small mushrooms and the
baby corn-on-the-cob into a small
bowl with 1 tbsp water. Cover the
bowl with pierced plastic wrap and
cook for 2 minutes on HIGH and set
aside. Combine all the ingredients for
the sauce in a glass measure. Cook
on HIGH for 3 minutes or until
thickened. Stir after 1 minute. Slice
the tofu into ½ inch slices. Drain the
black mushrooms and remove the
stalks. Drain the noodles and arrange
in 4 separate serving dishes. Add the
spinach, tofu, whole black
mushrooms and small mushrooms,
baby ears of corn, radish slices, and
lemon slices. Pour some of the sauce
over each serving and garnish with
the fresh chives. Heat the dishes
through for 1 minute on HIGH and
serve the remaining sauce separately.

Microwave
MAIN MEALS

INDEX

Dep. Leg. B-32315-87